GW00713249

Shy White Tiger
Richard W. Halperin

salmonpoetry

Published in 2013 by
Salmon Poetry
Cliffs of Moher, County Clare, Ireland
Website: www.salmonpoetry.com
Email: info@salmonpoetry.com

ISBN 978-1-908836-34-2

COVER PHOTOGRAPHY: *Jessie Lendennie*
COVER DESIGN: *Siobhán Hutson*

Printed in Ireland by Sprint Print

Salmon Poetry gratefully acknowledges the support of The Arts Council

For my parents

Acknowledgements

Acknowledgement is due to the editors of the following publications in which a number of these poems have appeared.

IRELAND: *Census: The Third Seven Towers Anthology, Cyphers, The Dublin Quarterly, Open Christianity Newsletter, The Poetry Bus, Poetry Ireland Review, Revival Poetry Journal, Ropes Unravelled, THE SHOp, Skylight 47, The Stinging Fly, The Stony Thursday Book No. 8, Translation Ireland 2013*. UK: *Ambit, Anon, Areté, Carillon, The Delinquent, 14 Magazine, The Frogmore Papers, Obsessed with Pipework, Orbis, Planet: The Welsh Internationalist, Poetry Review / The Poetry Society, Sentinel Champions*. FRANCE: *The French Literary Review, Upstairs at Duroc, Van Gogh's Ear*.

'Half Buried' makes reference to *Unravelling the Spiral—The Life and Work of Fred Conlon* (1943—2005) by Jack Harte (Scotus Press, Dublin, 2010). 'Our Cassie' was included in the book *Dogs Singing—A Tribute Anthology* edited by Jessie Lendennie (Salmon Poetry, 2010).

Two poems won first prizes in competitions: 'Snow Falling, Lady Murasaki Watching' (iYeats, Sligo, 2012) and 'Rubbings' (*New Tricks with Matches*, University College Dublin, 2012). Two won second prizes: 'The River 8' (*Sentinel Quarterly*, July 2011) and 'Blue Day' (Dromineer, 2010). Commended poems are 'Between the Spaces of the Song the Song Sang' (Dromineer, 2010), 'Dear Leo' (Wigtown, 2010), 'Ithaca' (Leaf Books, Abercynon, 2010), 'Where does the soul go when it goes?' (Ver Poets, St Albans, 2009). 'The Lady with the Toque Hat' was long-listed (Hungry Hill, Beara Peninsula, 2012).

Contents

Shy White Tiger

the postcard said. Siberian.
There he is, staring out
staring calm.
Someone stole his colour
but not his dignity.
Someone stole his colour
but not his beauty.
Someone stole his colour
and they can have it.
'What are you doing with yours, my friend?
When I shed blood, it's to eat.
When I walk, the grace of it makes God gape.
Each of us has something removed before arriving.
And more while here.
Then, everything.
And?'

Between the spaces of the song the song sang

The beautiful time the spring was gone.
Winter like a rumour of death

had gone south for the winter. There were
no people in the song or seals

splashing in the song or sounds in the song
of peppercorns cracking when crushed

or the 'Ah' a dictionary makes
when whoever writes it writes it

or Georgian mansions or barracks
in the song or fancy dress balls.

Only a child holding a balloon
string and a sky like a ribbon

waving. There was only the violet
ribbon of child and balloon and sky.

Brief, she was too young to know there
was no song in the song so she sang it.

Where does the soul go when it goes?

Where does the soul go when it goes?
to a hotel? to the flat white light
of an Edward Hopper painting?

Where does the soul go when it goes?
for a walk? for a cry?
I am not talking about death.

Death is a big bird, red, green, Brazilian.
A splashy thing. Waiting. Funeral. Ceremonies.
Heaven maybe. The soul is or isn't in that.

Where does the soul go when it goes?
when one is driving, reading but not reading,
listening but not listening, the vast vestibule

of inattention. When the motel is vacant,
curtains flapping. Anyone can enter, and many do.
(But who is responsible for damages?)

Where is the soul most of the time?
when there is no conversation,
only empty contraption?

when we were at breakfast an hour ago,
as hours go. Where were you?
Florida maybe.

Dream, waking thought

                                        Both.
A garden of pale blue roses, in moonlight,
At the back of a house. Walled. Quiet.
Some associations: the blue rose of forgetfulness,
Thief of Baghdad; Steve and Nat's
small walled garden in Cheltenham;
pale blue hydrangeas, my first certainty
as a child that I had been alive before I was born—
even to this day when I see in florists' shops
pots of hydrangeas (but they have to be
pale blue).

                Memory is a deceptive word.
What it is used for, the what, is not the past,
that would be like saying lake means
half a lake. One day I shall be again
where there are hydrangeas.

Dream, waking thought.
A garden of pale blue roses,
in moonlight. At the back of
a sleeping house.
Walled. Quiet.
Some dreams, most,
one has to make an effort
to remember, to write down correctly.
Not this one. Here it is.

The Two

My father and I were walking down a dusty road.
'Will my mother be waiting at the end?' I asked.

He taught me to fish, he tried to teach me gin rummy,
He took me to symphonies and hoped for the best.

We should be holding hands, I thought.
But of course we weren't.

How he felt about that, or about most things,
I never did know.

Questions, any at all, seemed hurtful.

He liked detail, concrete things, so wish I could mention some.

But experience merits being reported as is.
As is.

My father and I were walking down a dusty road.
'Will my mother be waiting at the end?' I thought I heard
    him say.

At that moment, and I think my wife understands,
I knew the utter sadness of love.

The Crepuscular Theory of Light

That light in its purest form is found
In jazz heard on a summer night;

That light is drinkable in any
Colour one chooses, as the mad know;

That we think light bends because we bend—
Racine knew better: it's a hatchet;

That where she lives now is a bossa
Nova of light, as when she lived here;

That just to think her name is an
Acceptable substitute for light.

Admiration in the Hospice

Hats in *Juliet of the Spirits*, how they float out or are poised
    upon
the heads of the dreamers, namely the heads of everyone,
that they are the souls of the dreamers—veils, feathers, nets,
a sturdy Chinese crown (Giulietta)—that this is what we really
    look like
if we could see it and that Fellini saw it and filmed it.

The observation of the narrator of *The Fall* that all lies are on
    their way
to truth, that in fact everything is, so in the end the lie is
    seen as a lie
and therefore loses importance as a lie and cannot be hidden,
thus the Fall and thus also Resurrection, Tolstoy but my pen
    slipped.

That to angels looking down we look like frisbees.

Our Cassie

The signs were up all over Glendalough for a year.
'Has anyone seen our Cassie?'

There followed
a brief description of the world's most lovable dog,
with faded colour snapshot to prove to anyone with eyes to see.

I read it. The valley shook (and not for the first time).
Years before, months after my wife, yes, had died—
ashes scattered, hugs received, wonderful letters reread,
phonecalls 'You OK?' levelling off—
I'd been walking thinking of nothing in particular; a boon, that;
when I got exactly the same impulse as Cassie's owners.
The only sensible thing to do, really.

Boy Left in a Car in the Pouring Rain

Windows up. No other quiet like it, this kind of inside.
Parents ducked out to buy something, then taking
Their time about it. Outside, rain on metal.
Inside the bubble: metal, stale velour, ashtrays, tucked maps.

What if they don't come back? Rain. Car. *What I think*
Is real isn't real, never was. Only the real is real:
Waiting in a car in the rain. It's like taking a nap in public.

'In the middle, in the middle' spoke—if rain on the roof can
    speak.

They were very bold to have gone off and left me,
Whoever they were. In the middle, all right. What I'd thought
Was me isn't. Waiting. Inside. Velour. Maps. I.

Back from the Bridge

You and I used to go
Toward the bridge
Toward the Pont du Carrousel
Of a Sunday
An easy goal
A weekend stroll
Cafés and quais behind
The Seine ahead
The sun above
The Louvre beyond
     gardens roofs windows
     a city a glow
Beyond the undertow.

Hand in hand
We used to go
Toward the pont
An easy goal
A weekend stroll
And pleasant.

But, barring accident,
Never can a couple go
Hand in hand
Across certain bridges.

And so.

And so two years ago
Cafés behind
The Seine below
The roofs beyond

Your hands outstretched
You crossed the flow
Into the sun
An easy goal
A weekend stroll
And distant

And I watched you cross and cross
Your hands outstretched
Your back aglow.

And there was no more bridge.
And I walked home alone.

Mont Blanc

The windows are open and nothing walks in.
If Shelley had thought that, he wouldn't have written
Anything. A breeze, no breeze, wish for a breeze,
Memory of breezes, are all breezes.
There are no such things as ghosts, Willie,
You can write better poems than that. (And he did.)
No death. Rub out—the better term. My mother
Was too alive ever to be dead, no
Languorous ghost, she. She wouldn't be
Having any of that. And there's Jesus with
His mouth full of food, as usual. The windows
Are open, or if closed you want to throw them
Open, which can't be done in winter. So,
You light a fire which is either a fire,
Or a good book, or a good glass, or a good look
At who's next to you or nearly—or who was.
Tenses are baggage, so out with them, out
The window with them.

The Order of Things

I wondered about angels,
where they were, where they are, angels.

I have heard, or thought I have heard,
the rustle of shoulders, the drawer
opening in the night, a fragrance now therein,
as when we say something wonderful that we haven't
thought of, as when you said to me 'Why not?'
and so we went out walking together
and you, not much later, regretted it
(but only sometimes, I keep telling myself)
and died much sooner than you would have
had you walked alone. 'No,' you say,
but I do not believe you.

                      I do not
wonder about that. 'You should,' you say,
and there is the smell of jasmine in the room,
although vetiver was your scent.
But I do wonder about angels, and
flares in the night that lit our way like fireflies.

Half Buried

A gravestone sculpture, so I took it to be,
in limestone by an Irish artist.
A young strong woman,
her effigy deliberately half-buried
in the surrounding dirt or grass
blanketlike tucked up to her chin.

His version of her,
as any artist's vision is a version.

Peaceful it looked
dreaming or dead
(Why do we have two words for that?)

She or it.
(Why do we have two words for that?)

Dirt or grass were playing their part,
since the artist had included them,
half covering the effigy, half not,
or two-thirds covering, one-third not—
dirt and grass, as they do,
shifting up and down,
down and up, with the days.

A work of art, a work of genius.
Quite possible, then,
that critics will argue
about how the grass behaves,
about what is the grass's *intention*,
as they argue about how artists behave,
or misbehave.

The effigy of Iníon Mhathu
by Fred Conlon (1943-2005)
photographed in a book by Jack Harte.
I was not in the graveyard, you see.
I was in the book,
I was in sepia,
pre-Genesis colour.

Reading the accompanying text
I learned that Mathu's Daughter
had walked the earth as ancient myth.
That the grounds she was now on
were Kiltimagh—
not, therefore, a graveyard
(one's views depending).

No graveyards since
seem correct,
everything too out
or too in.
Thank you, Mr Conlon, for that.

You had the eye of the pure in heart: the heart.

You had the madness of the artist:
You could not leave things
as they are without
raising them from where everyone
is used to thinking
they should only be.
Pray God similarly misbehave.

Who is in a poem?

A breeze comes through the window
And starts this this day:
I see my father in his darkroom,
Red light bulb on, a tray of developing fluid—
I can still smell it, like etherealised vinegar—
An image becoming into being on the sensitised
Paper in the tray, as he rocks oh so gently
The fluid. A wedding photo of the bride's mother,
Taken in the South Side of Chicago in 1954.
A large woman in a small white satin hat,
A proud woman, proud to have her portrait
Taken, an experienced matriarch sitting, just sitting,
Just breathing for a change, her ample bosom
Still, she still, not on but in
A wet white sheet of paper—until
The first ghost of her, then a more confident ghost, then
No ghost but She, there, as in amniotic fluid,
Dignified, submerged, in sepia. Waiting
To be clipped by my father with metal clips
On a line, hung clipped on a line
Not so much to dry—her skin is moist, rich—
as to be, in that thick mat magic paper.

No poem can do better. A shroud
Sometimes can, a serviette with a lipstick stain on it
Sometimes can, an upside-down image on the retina
Sometimes can, the kiss of God known only
As an interruption (did I feel it?) of its
Usual absence from the ventricles of the heart
Sometimes can—a sepia kiss let's call it, why not?—
Inside our pitch dark. A red light bulb going,
No one yet having tugged hard the string of it.

Strawberry Jam

It was always on the breakfast table
With my mother my father and me

During sunshine and frost on the windowpane
The radio Patti Page Korea

During arguments during silences

Sticky
Red
Delicious

Sometimes ignored
One time thrown

It and I witnesses

To what?
Mornings marriage Earth

Things taken for granted

Each atom of it years ago split

Nothing left except

Blinding white light

Gobs of love

My Dad's Last Days

i. *My dad*

Not Doric. Didn't fall in battle, shield clanging.
Doesn't need to be clothed as myth.
Any dad is myth enough.
There are only two kinds anyway: good dads and crap ones.
Mine was the former.
Tee shirts, jeans, pointless to say more,
You've got your own to think about.

ii. *How he lived*

Well, none of your business, actually; and barely mine.
The afterlife wasn't among his values, but privacy was.
He lost that, too, toward the end.

iii. *His last days*

He could have been killed instantly in a car crash forty years
    prior
while coming home from having played his best game of golf ever.
But he wasn't; he drew the short straw.
So, pain, humiliation, protest, rage, tears, weakness, passivity.
Here he fell asleep.
He was my dad, so all these times counted; and none.

My Mother's Gravestone

There isn't one.
What dates or phrases could contain her?

The Lady in the Toque Hat

The lady in the toque hat
with a jaunty feather

on a park bench every day
in my neighbourhood sixty-five years ago.

Old. Small. Very elegant.
Romanian someone said.

Would watch the birds the children
would sometimes talk to other old ladies

then she would go home.

I would be on my tricycle
with a parent or two.

'No it's not her job,' my mother explained,
'she likes doing this.'

I sit in the park most days.
Now I understand the feather.

After an Encounter with a Connemara Pony

Have you ever looked into the eyes
Of a so-called animal and seen
Someone more intelligent than you
Staring right back? Think about it. Two
Writers, Barrett and Woolf, choose to make
Immortal the cocker spaniel Flush;
Jack Yeats, past grief, gobs a great cream horse
Comforting a blue broken man, dubs
It 'My Beautiful, my Beautiful';
Rembrandt's 'Flight into Egypt,' Tours, France,
Catches by matchlight Mary, Jesus,
Irritable, preoccupied, while
Their mount, a jackass, beatific,
Leads them through vales; then there's that white whale.
No conclusions, just questions which spark
When points of light reflect back in eyes
Not ours as through a live glass darkly.

Circus of the Perfume of Time

i. *Rainy Sunday in Paris*

My small flat, some crumbled pieces of toast,
a friend ill in Toronto, sound of rain on geranium pots,
an extra jumper on, a mug of tea, a letter to you forming,
maybe this one, a hand in mine maybe yours,
a book instead, but one can do worse,

a genius writing, Charlotte Brontë, and all Paris
like a square of cheap Velcro is ripped away—underneath,
the heartbeat and miraculous guts of a small strong woman.
In the stone court below, squeals of children happy or morose
just back from church day, circus day, anyway, Sunday.

Rain lashing my window in a beat, beat, beat,
nothing is small, nothing was small, nothing is small.
A hand in mine maybe yours. An hour forming.
Rainy Sunday in Paris. By Monday a piece of crumbled toast,
memory of cherry jam.

ii. *Room in the Light of a Remembrance*

Wooden shutters open, windows at their angles open
onto a quiet court. The sun somewhere, like a sack
of wheat. Summer nine a.m., I in a chair, the air there
and not there, wheaten light only. Light is where
the pictures, where the photos, should be,
the glare of light on glass in frames and so
no pictures. Some furniture (no need to name which,
there isn't much), not needing light or air. Brown,
familiar, chosen long ago by no one around lately,
weighing the room down like lead blocks
a fallen sail on grass in a windy place.
It is not my room, I am negotiable.

A street away, church bells ring, Sunday
summer nine a.m., an angelus slid backward
into a mass of blue cloth and, so, negligible. A fly,
of a million different colours convenient
to label blue, flies in one window, glances off
the refrigerator door and flies out, easy about
the day, the time, the place. 'Write,' I tell myself
but decide not to, there will be no bite to it, no who
no what, only a dislodged where from wherever
where is not negotiable. I move from one chair
to another chair and say the only prayer
that makes a prayer: Why not? 'Write,' I tell myself—
but it must be in black ink on lined yellow paper
because that is what seems to be required
by the inertia of light and I a piece of furniture
brought long ago by no one around lately
and so I do and this is it.

iii. *Some Sundays Are Like That*

I am in France reading a Russian book translated into English.
It is not Fate that has laid down these three cards
for me slap, slap, slap, but rather the other she
has done it who walks into the room.
I can't tell if the motes in the air are sprigs
on her dress or summer on her skin,
there is too much light and movement.
She touches my shoulder, I look up

from words, people, towns, dusty roads, intrigues,
to not words but word, which is her way.
'They're playing tennis in the park
just outside the window,
any child's alive more than you.
If you're waiting for big bronze doors
to swing open, think again.

You don't have to play tennis like a teenager
not to need to play tennis. Go out
through the door that we painted
when we first moved in, it's not yet too swollen,
you'll be in the Luxembourg Gardens,
as usual.'

So I did and am. It was she who'd
shuffled, cut and dealt me all my cards
and all of her own, every last one, which is
the difference between love in a book
and marriage, reader.

iv. *Around the Candle*

Around the candle in the dark bedroom
a little circus of shadow and flame: horses,
striped poles, queasy trapezes, lots of
other spangled things, children's laughter surely,
children's fears more to the point really.
Snap of flame, trick of shadow.

A hairy hand stretched out from Uranus maybe
to light the wick just before sleep, his;
and so, we for a while.

Willow Pattern

Blue on white. What it meant
When first designed—like anything,
Including oneself—is barely remembered.
Lake. Temple. Garden. Bridge,

Three figures crossing it; a willow,
Far too big, its leaves like spades,
Like an adolescent's hands,
Drooping near to it.

In the air, two birds, beak to beak.
A world complete,
On a plate, on a cup,
On a serving dish.

When feet walk through my empty
House—and they will—which
Will they see? What part of the picture
Do I want to be? Lake. Temple,

Garden. Bridge. One of the
Two birds, you the other.
Don't disturb that, visitor.
The Trojan War was fought for less.

Carl

Told everyone I'd be away for four days but I never came back.

Notes slipped under the door including hers but so what
police called
door kicked in
window still jammed shut, as if that meant anything.

Hha! Not here, am I?

Shoot me full of this
placate
massage
plead
browbeat
finally give up.

Hha! Not here. Could have told you that.

I'll be back when I damn well feel like it.

On vacation.

White Nights

Sometimes starry winter nights tilt,
As in a dream of Dostoevsky's,
A madman on the deserted streets of Saint Petersburg
Only it's a farm field, fenceless in the cold white light
And a dog running toward you,
Friendly, happy to see you,
Yes, your dog, the one you loved when you were five,
And the field tilts, or is it the stars that tilt,
And the dog running toward you not through the field
But through the mass of stars, so so so many,
And you feel you're close to what's really home,
Home without houses, without—thank God—memory,
Without anything more than a feeling of warmth,
Of love, nothing else was necessary,
Never was quite real, and there's the dog
Getting closer across the stars, across the field,
Across the deserted streets of Saint Petersburg
And you try to close the book or you will die of happiness,
And the harder you try to close the book, you open the book
More and more open, hoping memory won't come into it,
Hoping everyone you ever loved will be there, without memory,
Only with love, and these are white nights, nights
Without end, without colour, with only the sense that
Dogs and horses have when they know—know know know—
That something good is very near and warm, and
Dawn blows away like a coloured rag
And so does happiness, because this is happiness.

Fondly Fat-Kneed Jeanne Margaret, in Memoriam

The old lady on the street
Carrying two shopping bags.
Not who is she? Or what
Is she carrying? Rather, is she me?

One needn't be reborn
To have other lives, this is
All of them now.
(Thoughts at four in the morning.)

The body is an ink pot.
But the body itself is also ink,
It runs in the rain,
That is why there is rain.

One is trapped in one's head
By a head cold, so can't escape to notice.
Cities are the worst head colds.
(Except at four in the morning).

Noon. I am on the street.
I may be the old lady. She totes her bags,
Cassiopeia gets varicose veins,
My legs hurt.

Do people who kill
Know they are committing suicide—
Or do they have to wait to die
To find that out?

Some, not I, can feel this all the time.
When I was six and she four,
We were sitting on a stone fence
On the strand at Ballycastle,

Sea—sun—spray—
She wearing plum, I plum.
'What would you like
Most in the world?' I asked.

'Someone to scratch my back,'
She said. She must have
Already been
Very close to heaven.

Ithaca

What were we talking about before I
fell asleep? Oh, yes. How *The Odyssey*
was a good tale well told. That an odyssey is a
return home. About the absurdity of the body
and three cheers for that. About your
rupture with your best friend and whom
that hurt the more. About how your mother
despite your mother was your mother,
and stuck with that, and you stuck all over
with, yes, love for her, like surgical glue,
and about how if one pries the letters of 'insomnia'
apart, 'mother' would be in-between each one of them,
and we arguing, 'ah, but small m or capital M?'
and laughing at that and there went your mother.
About how beds are in themselves cold
and what a good idea on someone's part toes are.
Or were we talking in my sleep after
all these years? I reach for you and you aren't.
An hour or so ago's our only island now.

The Liffey, 22 December 2006

On the millennium bridge at midnight and squinting,
You don't need Venice—
The custom house bobbing, the ha'penny arch, the blurry lights

On the millennium bridge at midnight and remembering,
You don't need the Red Sea—
Nearby a city of crumbly red bricks
Baked under duress

On the millennium bridge at midnight and half-discerning
    Ur of the Chaldees off the north quay,
You don't need protection against muggers—
They think you're crazy

On the millennium bridge at midnight,
Doges, dentures, dunces floating underneath,
You don't need—
Dublin, actually

The Double

He was waiting for me on the stairs, my double,
or he was in a hurry and in an absent moment passed me.

Sometimes when I talk, more often when I listen,
I am he and so remember imperfectly what was said, but
    he remembers.

'Three pounds for these?' I asked the girl. 'What are you asking?'
she said, 'you just bought the same from me an hour ago.'

Sometimes, it is true, I am out of focus, but that is not he.
He is on his own, my double.

When you found me and stayed, when our lives went hand in hand
by I know not what slippage, when we were and seemed to have
    always been—

even then I sometimes thought, she thinks I am *he*.
I never asked you if you knew I had a double,

which proves to me that I am not a moral person.

When I saw him once while shaving, I said to myself, she knows,
it is *he* she first saw, it is *he* she loves,

but she's a moral person, she'll stick it out to the end.
Which you did.

Are three pounds plus three pounds six pounds or three pounds?
You never were good at maths, thank God.

Have to stop now. I'm crying.

A Confidence

A man sat next to me on a
park bench and started talking
and it was winter and I
couldn't stop him. 'They studied,'
he said, 'every photograph
ever taken of the earth
and every photograph ever
taken ever, since before
Daguerre, they put them,' he said,
'all into a computer,
they ran,' he said, 'a programme
written by that genius they
keep locked up inside a
mountain in the Caucasus,'
he said, 'and do you know what
they found, do you know what they
found, they found that the earth looks
like, looks exactly like—they
matched it—a blob of light as
reflected at night in a
hare's eye. But they're keeping it
a secret because no one would
believe it.' But—then he left—
I believe it.

Hunter College, 1964

Girls bright bright bright
rushing down arsenic-
green corridors
handbags glasses
pencils the pill
paystubs (most worked)
spiral notebooks
Hobbes Hölderlin
Marx Martha Graham
Arroyo Auden
mid-Manhattan
Hunter!

In classrooms
questions
in cafeteria
love and friendship
gales of laughter
girlfriends boyfriends
dissected down
to the last
kidney twitch.

Down corridors
like electric moths
one of them blue:
you. Later

the college went co-ed
something gained
something displaced
and spinning
past Saturn now.

The Girl on the Hill

The mists lift, and there's a girl on the hill.
No, don't open the shutters. You'll lose it.
Sound, sight, taste, smell, touch, yes, are sense.
But so is waiting. Borders, bullies, competition
Collapse like rotten wood. So do bluebells and hope.
Everything has a weak side. (God's is mercy,
Bernadette observes.) Is it the girl who waits,
Or the hill? Either could have been in the
Contraption of hell or heaven when it fell.
I speak of the empirical. How many tears
Does it take to make one drop of the empirical?
Tears move. The mists lift, and—no, don't open
The shutters—there's a girl on the hill, at evening.

Windows

Where is she when you need her?
The city is the city
offices, jostling, buses, buzz
theatres, museums, cabs
discos, nuns, execs, hospitals
Bleecker Street, Bill Evans, Blossom Dearie, Monk

what curves aligns just once and you can see through it
a window beyond a window beyond a window
the glass staircase flattens
and beyond there's
little Miss Gone Missing
the city girl
the urban chick
who was so part of it
the blue note
in the blue crowd
in the blue room
the sixtieth cigarette
the fifth espresso
where life gets good at three a.m.
the baggy-eyed at ease girl

there's she
walking
just walking
on a hill
in the countryside
beyond the last pane
walking easy
leading animals up a hill
into a barn
and through the barn
and out the other side
to heaven.

On Revisiting the Lifework of Joseph Cornell, 1903–1972

For Theresa Nicholas

This is the New York out of time.
This is the New York I lived, that was there.
This is the New York 'scaped the wandering rocks
of greed. This is the New York of souls.
This is the New York of the perceptions.
This is the New York of pure dignity.
This is the New York of pure privacy.
This is the New York of worms, angelic moths.
This is my mother's New York, of designs.
This is my wife's New York, nests of artists.
This is my friends' New York, the town of pals.
This is the New York of dead grey money.
This is the New York of window breezes.
This is my New York. Thank you, Joseph.

Off Bantry

i. *Closing up*

You folded blankets and put them in the armoire.
There was a grace in that and no surprises.
You folded sheets, dried in Whiddy Island sun.
You pressed them with your hands, there was no need of ironing.

We were closing up the rented summer house,
Leaving it for the next ones—dusting, swabbing,
Replacing, locking the clean windows,
Moving as two solids through the solids of the house,
Moving as one soul through the souls of the house,
For there had been many souls and there would be the next ones
(And during one bad moment I had been many souls),
Moving through the bad and good moments of the house—
The yard outside with its daily sheep droppings
Because of gaps in the fence, blue sky and white clouds above.

Fresh flowers are better than dried flowers any day,
Except when pressed into the pages of a book,
The words on the page written, sold, not changing, *there*,
The dried flower (a cornflower, in our case) also *there*
But infinitesimally changing, desiccating, browning at the edges
Like the paper of the pages and hats off to that.

What is done between two people can never be undone.
What is said between two people can never be unsaid,
To try to change in the mind what happened
Is to block transfiguration.

You were upstairs folding sheets that smelled of sun.
I left out on a table a tacky summer book.
No one would ever press a flower into it. Or would they?
Who knows what things can happen in houses?

ii. *Cowbells*

'Do cows still wear them?'
you'd asked. We were not
near Klosters. So, 'No.'
We were on Whiddy Island
where the cows are wild.
Their ears twitch.
Their . . . who cares? We
were together, homing—
road, hill, house.
Long time ago.

'Was this your house?'
Serge asked, a friend
in pilgrimage.
I couldn't speak, which was
the same as 'yes.'
Two storeys, white,
red the trim, green the yard
and brown.
Someone—a couple again?—
lives there all the time now:
sheets, shirts, trousers,
flapping on plastic strings
in open Irish air.

'Cowbells somewhere?'
he asked.
Day, that's sure, day ballooning
like a shirt faded clean
by sun and wind. Hill, house.
A smell of bed.
Not Klosters. But cowbells.
Yes, cowbells.

Photographers

They take pictures of pictures.
    ducks monuments garbage relatives
Pictures of the picture of the night
Pictures of the picture of earth as seen from the picture of the
    moon and vice-versa
Click

There are no pictures of places, only
Of pictures of pictures of places

There are only pictures of time
Time in a face a carrot a city
Click

All photographers are therefore cruel
All photos are therefore noble

All photographers are therefore noble
All photos are therefore cruel

As Hamlet said, 'Say Cheese.'

Blue Day

We were there the day the great fear left us.
We were in a sailboat in the middle of a lake.
The waters, which had devoured us,
Worse, which had threatened to devour us,
Worse, which threaten to devour us,
Fell calm, blue, green, bright, kind.
We cared about the sun.
We had stopped sailing, because where were we going?
We did not care what was above the sun.
We did not care what swam under us or waited.
Light was no longer the mirror, we were the mirror.
We knew that sounds had been a kindness,
That that's what the wind, the rip of trees,
The mountains torn from their sockets,
The sift and suck of anthills spiralling like sand spouts,
The sharp inhale of the maniac,
Had meant.
We were no longer afraid of brilliance.
A heart beat, it didn't have to, and we laughed at that,
And as we laughed, the fear left us.
There was a smell of olive trees from beyond the water and sand,
And cries of birds whom nothing would ever kill now
And their astonishment at that,
And a curled leopardess breathing the sleep of sabbath,
And dry cracked ground not minding being dry for a while
Because that's how things are.
All was pause, sun, boat, sail.
It had always been only that, waiting.
No more terror waiting.
The rest had been a picture, ourselves a picture.
Only pain and love had been real,
One of them now no longer there.
We together—that's what day is—that day.

Before Two Portraits of My Mother (version), ca. 1900, by Emile Nelligan

My mother! I love her in this old painting
Done in her glory days when she was young.
Her head gleams like a lily, her gaze is brilliant,
Scintillating like a Venetian mirror.

No more the same, now, here, her, my mother.
Wrinkles have creased the beautiful marble brow.
She's lost the flash of that tender time
When her bridal song sashed her like a poem written in roses.

To compare today makes me sad in two doses:
This face, haloed in joy; this face, hollowed by care.
Sun bright, dense fog, gathering unto the end of years.

But . . . how little of the heart the heart can make clear!
How is it I can smile at these lips so worn, faded, ill?
How is it I can weep at a portrait that is smiling still?

Family Circle

Outside in the darkness, Lake Michigan, not the ryefields of
　　Elisabethgrad.

Uncle Rudy played the violin.
Mrs Rudy, Min,
used to being neglected, asserted her existence by a sort of
　　irritated goodness.
Aunt Julia, wife unto Aaron, presided; cards; French magazines;
　　lunches with the Judge; great-grandchildren itemized;
　　Unitarianism.
Aaron sometimes listened, sometimes slept.
Edna, the maid for fifty years, served brownies.
Uncle George quoted from his book on Tolstoy, Dostoevsky and
　　Turgenev, mainly for my benefit.
My grandfather spoke of having sung in a boy's choir at court
　　for Alexander II.
Grace, my step-mother from Missouri, gamely breasted the waves,
　　her day as a social worker recounted; her mother's having
　　just taken up oil painting.
I tried to disappear, then changed my mind: the only two clauses
　　of the contract of being a child.
Leo, my father, mortally wounded but good for another thirty
　　years, held us all together by sarcasms, which I viewed
　　(correctly) as kindness in fancy dress.

And beyond the huge black windows high above Lake Shore Drive
Chicago slept and worked and partied,
and Stalin and Truman and God outside pressed their noses against
　　the glass,
and I knew that my father would have admitted them
to the family circle,
or at least would have thought seriously about it,
had he been sure that at least one of them
could have drawn Min out
just a little more.

Sanatorium

i. *Magic Mountain*

I was sitting on the terrace
of a sanatorium in the cold
high air, reading *The Magic Mountain*,
other patients playing cards.

Reading and cards and cold high air—
mirrors flashing in a mirror.
Mann was no fool, I thought,
cranks and lovers, lovers and cranks,
everything else a magic trick—
look over there!—to distract.

I thought of a lovely serious girl,
Jean Simmons in a film of a sanatorium,
well-tailored in plaid silk, in artificial light,
other patients playing cards,
she elsewhere, walking undistracted
into the uncanny with her lover
for the ten minutes that comprise forever.
Maugham was no fool, I thought,
bad lungs make one think.

I was sitting on the terrace
of a sanatorium, reading *The Magic
Mountain*, when the greasy cards
that is all the mind is, slipped,
and I saw you, in high-collared black silk,
walking at a distance, the deep red sun
settling behind the mountains,
as far below a wasp
(one could hear it in that air)
carried the day away and ate it.

ii. *Green Sun*

I was in a very clean room.
No you nearby, no parents,
no lost friends, no other side
that I could sense.

I noticed the sun outside,
through the glass window
(no, most windows
are not of glass).

It was bright green, the sun.
That seemed correct.
I don't know why I'd
never noticed it before,
the window itself reflected it.

I woke up (let's say).
There was the sun as usual,
incorrect.

Did Alice in her dream
see a green sun?
I think that's all she saw.
I think she made up the rest
to avoid telling her sister.

Green sun.
It never is anything else.

I think animals know it.
It's only we
who don't know how to see.

Rabboni

He was probably wearing a wide hat
His face and hands were probably a bit burnt, considering
In his satchel a spade, possibly
On his feet anyone's sandals

As always in appearance
Hairy smooth plump scrawny short tall taller
The eldest and the runt of the litter
Pug ugly, certainly

His sack of seeds should have been the giveaway, but wasn't

What was?

As with all gardeners from Adam onward
His authority in providing to the as yet unenlightened
The distinguishing name:

Rhubarb root
Nasturtium
Summer bug early
Mole hole
Red fox paw print

mary

Book of Genesis

'Thus was heaven and earth finished with all their apparel.'
So Tyndale wrote. Nothing was attached yet.
All was as in a dream, bushes floated, or nearly.
Then a mist rose and out of the mist . . . .
So, the dream which had come out of a dream
And was recorded by a dreamer, ended.
Everything got tacked down.
That it had been a dream's the perfection of it:
It—what we breathe, live, see, step on, fight with, sleep
    under—
Sometimes is not there. When we blink; or think.

Before this genesis,
Was only the harm
That dreams have,
Not our familiar harm.
Only the devoured and the devouring
Recurring arm in arm,
An intimacy of relationship
That love is cousin to.

Today's the 1st of May 2009 in Paris.
I look out my window.
I read Tyndale, a poet strangled.
I drink my coffee.
I remember last night's dreams (fairly ugly).
No need to turn on the radio news
To hear the latest horrors
Of the species who found it necessary
To invent radio.
I start to say 'Hello earth.'
But the words stick. False peace.
Hello cords tugging at the pegs.
Hello sound of a heartbeat, re-
Membering its cousins.

Mountains of the Blue Haze

Our town is in the mountains.
Most times we take no notice,
most times we walk, talk,
listen, live, without thinking—
of what is walled out, of what
is walled in, of what
is a wall, a blue curtain
or green or brown,
light depending.

Like any stone, porous.
The top of an island the sea
once had covered, the island's
pushing up now, we near the top of it,
circled by our obsessions. Where
we were placed, a valley,
palm of the hand, a far country
which is how Freud describes
the human mind.

                    Cows,
goats, outhouses, our corrupt
mayor. Hatreds over land
which is only the sea
made vertical a while.
Genji visiting a old priest
in a hut, or maybe Genji
is the priest, time
doing such things.

Thin blue air,
to be seen on any vase, out
any window, in the eyes
of a teacher who notices
one's gifts, and the tenderness

of the hurt of that,
Mrs Lerner when I was twelve,
no Blake angel
could have done more.

Audible in bushes,
in caves, a tiny voice 'I am'
heard quite clearly
by Bernadettes and Chopins
and Raphael's dog.

Rumours of death, then
in our own sitting rooms death,
the body an unplugged machine,
questions only then arising,
we encircled by questions—
curtains or stones.

Our town is in the mountains.
Most times,
minds mangled by offices,
we do not notice.
Sometimes,
someone writes a poem—
Yeats or Eliot
or Li Po—
which is a blessing,
we in the mountains correctly,
the middle distance.

*Pablo, when I was ten
and you my step-father for a while,
you gave me Peru.
What can I give to you now?*

Pink Roses

Pink roses on the wallpaper of my nursery.
The bars of my crib white enamel,
I looking through them at frost on the windowpane,
Bright light of winter morning.

Night had been night, all right,
Monsters stalking inside and outside my head.
I thought they might have been friendly, actually.
I thought they might have come to be near the roses.

My parents were about in the next room.
Then one of them left, down the hallway.
The radio in the kitchen
Had not yet been turned on.

Through the wall I heard one sob.
Couldn't tell whose it was.
Sobs when there can only be one of them
All sound alike.

Rubbings

It has been
drizzling for hours. Does anyone know
what drizzle is? even saying 'drizzle is'
is drizzle, as if one were in a cloud, as if
there the familiar things are, but all in
fine drops, no change in sound, no sound
like the rain makes, but just a new companion.

When I was twenty I wrote a story 'Where
Is Glinka?' which no one understood because
there wasn't quite enough of it, but it
comforted me, as if it were rubbing itself
against my leg, as if I'd fallen asleep with
my pen in my hand and there was Glinka
and a sleigh and a transition, almost grey,

as between Alice's parlour and through
the looking glass, gauze she said it was like.
Agatha Christie when she was an old lady
wrote that yes she was religious and what a
fundamental value daily kindness had for her,
and that every day she read from Imitation
of Christ, and that after she was dead

what would happen to her would be
someone else's bother. It has been drizzling
for hours, nothing is going anywhere,
just fine drops suspended, and Glinka
rubbing himself against my leg, and someone
is telling a story by the fire, by the fire,
and before I fall asleep thank you Miss

Christie, Christie has a nice sound
to it, Miss separates off from it, Miss
has nothing to do with it any more.

Aunt Min Behind a Window

Across the courtyard and several buildings away,
Rue d'Estrées. An impression. Like a passport fingerprint,
Like a wine stain on a mahogany table.

Russian childless great-aunt Min,
Who passed most of her life
A few streets from Lake Michigan,

Before ending, as many do, in California.
Min in Paris.
Where she never was.

Without Uncle Rudy, which she seldom was.
With her brow furrowed, which it always was,
Even when she was at peace,

As if to demonstrate to her husband and older brothers
That she was thinking. That she was more than
The stupid little Manyushka

(But a marvellous cook) they all took her for.
A few trembly
Autumn leaves from an intervening plane tree

Slightly block my view on this day.
Afternoon. November. Poppy Day.
A sense of her hair

Frizzy and dark, as it was into her seventies.
Her eyes behind her glasses ever the eyes
Of a very good housekeeper, of a very good observer of

Other people's children.
What does she want of me?
Does she miss me?

Is she proud of me?
Is this like Dora in *David Copperfield*?
Does she want to hold my pens?—I at my desk,

Engrossed in my writing, old, far from Chicago?
One of those days when the grey Paris glare
Hurts the eyes.

Might she be at peace?
It might be like this. Min's version
Of peace.

Sleepy City

Paris six AM 10 September 2005
A frightened woman walking her whippet across the rue de
 Bourgogne
A lad on a bike not knowing what to be nervous about next
Rooks and crows carrying red pieces of yesterday's rat
A baker blinking flour
The quais the dead Louvre the Tuileries
A girl running in her underwear an old man too
 the latest ostriches of rich cities
Rumours of a head of state dying in Val-de-Grâce
Rumours of the rabid brontosaurus the other side of the Atlantic
Seventeen people in all skittering across the grey lake of Paris
 dawn
God self-smeared with ashes at what is done in His Name
Invisible temporarily against grey air grey morning glories
 grey grass
Benign with the relief of it
The right world beginning to peel itself away from the wrong one
Sleepy city
Before the coma of the day begins, Mr President

Muguet Day

Journal entry, Saturday, 1 May 2004:
To be a prophet in your own country is profitless,
To be a prophet in another's country is also profitless;
Which is worse only God and your doggie can say.
It's *muguet* day.

The long days begin in Paris. The world leaves its apartment,
Almost drunk with the beauty and the luck of a perfect day for
    muguets.
The sky sky blue, the clouds soft, the sun kind, the air
    suspiciously pure,
The traffic minimal, the time optimal,
The earth firm, the lawns shocking green, the grey pebbles clean
From last night's rain, the cracks of a very bad workweek healed.

Muguets everywhere, to sell, to buy, to give, to love, to lose,
    to keep for a while,
Bought for a reason or for no reason, enjoyed, seen, heard—
The peep and the perk of each bunch. *Muguet* day!

I take my walk as usual, the same weekend route, but today I'm in
A drop, the drop of the first of the pearly long Paris days
After winter had so long closed in. Goofs playing football,
Daddies pushing babies, mommies discussing Descartes and divorce,
Bikes, skateboards, doggies on and off the leash,
The old in couples or alone or alone alone,
The young in couples or alone or alone alone,
The whole world out walking, pausing at traffic lights or for
    no reason,
Stunned by the silly shock of a perfect day, *muguet* day.

I pass the house that is 243 boulevard Saint-Germain into which
Pauline Viardot moved after the deaths of Louis Viardot,
Turgenev, Wagner, George Sand, and their standards, the house
    with her eyebrows

Still raised in 1910 amused aghast at the very bad start of the
   new century.
The house shrugs like a cat in a puddle of sun, and I pass,
Dozens pass, hundreds pass, on *muguet* day.

I head for the centre, the Seine ridiculously beautiful
Which may be how glory looks, a million broken mirrors
Struck by the sun and flowing, people walking the banks,
People sitting on the stone steps leading into the flow,
The ducks floating, the bridges blinking in the light, the Pont
   des Arts
Bearing extra weight of picnickers picnicking on it
For no reason, for every reason, on *muguet* day.

The long day lengthens, the sky still perfect blue,
The breeze mild as the face of the zoo tiger in the 1879
   photograph
In a gallery window on the rue de l'Université, the caught
Moment just before the raw meat, or the nap, a stare in black
And white from a shop glass on this *muguet* day.

At evening, the sun still well up at nine o'clock, street-long
Shadows stripe the long lawn that is the avenue de Breteuil
As I pause, nearly back home. Young goofs
Play their football in the falling light, and will clearly play on
Until pitch dark. A white shaggy mutt,
Of the kind only an owner—and everyone else—could love
Pants up to me, then trots away, for profit
Or for no profit, on *muguet* day.

And so, a day: a drop, plump, glistening, a civilization
On the brink of stupid and avoidable destruction,
A sketch on onionskin, crumpled into a ball,
For some reason, for no reason, and kicked by yet another goof
On his way to a second of May.

The River 8

O lordy I'm going
downstream the fingertips
still hold onto the stone I was
taught to hold onto
let my knuckles get white
as the stone you'll breathe
I'll swim on up to the great Up To
and so I held onto but not
the stone the stone detached
like Canada (underestimate
me and I'll burn down
the White House again) and we're
on to bluegreenlands
bluegreenhands bluegreenblue
reptilian light Yours lordy
I and the stone that let go
(and when I say to the stone
what about *that* it says sorry
thought I was a member but
I just had consultative status)
and past us in the flow
I see let go avenue de villars
roscoe avenue chicago
dorotheergasse wicklow since
(I hope this is like marriage
the beginning and the end hardly
count only the so-long
middle) no address is home
downtown downstream
so let's go home lordy since
you're the stone let's go
home together

Blue Bottle

You used to trick sparrows
at the Landmann Café
into coming into your hand
to take bread—
only, there was no bread.

They would look beady-eyed,
and fly away furious.
'They're spherical enough already,'
you would say.

And that was our day
at the Landmann Café
in Vienna.

Bluebottle bluebottle bluebottle fly
delicate dainty
purplegreen sheen
walking on the ceiling
like an upside-down eye
(two wings make a fly fly
one wing makes a fly flail
three wings make a fly fey
and that is the theology
of a fly)

There in the morgue
on the sheet
on the feet
on the crown
on the two long-stemmed yellow roses
your sister laid upon you

What can a fly carry away?
what so tiny?
what so light?
what so flash of hue?

less than a crumb
less than a molecule
of jasmine

the biggest souls don't weigh very much

bluebottle bluebottle bluebottle blue
there he goes with you

you did not fool him this time.

Lucerne

As we went deeper into the forest, 'Leo,' I said,
'we've lost our way.' 'My name's Edward,' he said,
'after the change.' 'Is it your name we've lost then
or the way? aren't you my dad?' 'Sometimes,' he said,
'Have you the cake? They won't be expecting it.'
'Yes,' I said, voice cracking, for it hadn't changed yet.
'Good,' he said, 'take the next left, I left the keys in the car. Bye.'

Why do trees only speak Chinese if you're not Chinese?
Where did Chicago go? I saw the Buddha crossing Wabash Avenue.
Isn't Glenmalure over that ridge?
If they waved to me from the helicopter why couldn't they see me?
What if they don't like the icing? well, it's the thought
    that counts.
Just lie down, might warm up if I curl up.

Let's see.
Mother was I ere I saw Elba.
All Gaul is divided into three prawns.
Is this really the way to Lucerne?
Is this really the way to Lucerne?
Is this really the way to Lucerne?
If they waved to me from the helicopter why couldn't they see me?

We went out

We went out because that's where we were going.
We went out to do what we were going to do.
The news had come that you were dead.
The news had come and were we happy or glad.
The end had come of all that suffering.
The end had come of cursing God or loving God.
We were in the middle because we were in the middle.
Where we had been carried where we had been born.
We went out because because because because.
We went out because that's where we were going.
We went out to do what we were going to do, Harry.

The Floating Book

For James Hilton

There, open to
I don't know which two pages

as it were—but almost—
on a library table

light hitting it
through big glass windows

für Elise? for Paula?
can't quite read it.

This poem is, I think, in it,
from it, as are all my others

the recent ones anyway.
They say that just at death

the amnesia begins to lift,

or before
as when Hess plays Bach

or Callas sings Lucia
or Plato thinks.

Halls. Rooms.
Light, but brighter.

Cries from just beyond the hill:
'No hurry. We're here.

You left behind your book.
Gather from it meanwhile

your random harvest.'

The Return

An agèd sage gently rides an ox.
The reins are held by a servant
Who guides the ox and sage to the left.
The night goes this way, the stars go that way.
The lake goes this way, the waters go that way.
The three travellers continue their journey,
Until the picture is without them.

On the wooden dock of a riverbank,
A woman stands waiting for her husband.
She has forgotten his name,
And she herself never had a name.
In her hand she holds a letter:
I am blind now, so now I am sure
I shall find my way back to you.
She folds the letter and puts it back
In her book, the pages of which are blank,
The cover of which consists of one word
That long ago she wrote with her best ink
In a bold hand: 'Comfort.'

Passing, passing

Two students lie on their backs on a riverbank talking,
Their caps pushed back, their arms over their eyes
To protect their eyes from the sun, the river flowing,
The clouds unseen passing, passing. I will do this
And I will do that, one says. I will do this and I
Will do that, the other says. Each talks as if to himself,
That intimate, that unformed, that easy, because friends
Forever, their books in satchels on the grass, the river flowing,
The summer nearly over, the afternoon any afternoon,
As if there will be infinite afternoons, as if the sun were
A third friend, as if there were no difference between day
And drowsiness, as if there were no towns or obligations.

Later, much later, dying and very old—they had taken
Different paths, of course—one of them, the one who didn't
Die at forty-five—sees himself on the riverbank again,
He and his friend talking, planning, letting the day run through
Their fingers, because why should the future ever come?
'That was perfection,' he thinks. 'That the future was a story
We could sketch and discard, sketch and discard,
Our voices murmuring, our books in our satchels, our caps
Pushed back, all the ropes loosed and not our concern, really.
Maths is not perfection, perfection is not perfection,
Perfection is what music points to, the next note not there yet
And so not our concern yet, but surely something wonderful
Wherever it is going, and we were there, wherever it was going,
Wherever it was going.'

Birches on a Day

I walked through them in the usual dappled light,
They not turning but I, in the light, turning
Toward birches, as deeper and quieter I went,
Not falling but walking toward the cave where
Greenness lives. I'd known this wood before—over there
Under a tree (not a birch) Tolstoy reading
And Repin painting him reading, an old man
In loose white holding a book raised toward the light
That one associates with birches, I not in
Loose white and in fact I not—coming alone
From church after our wedding or whatever
The ceremony had been, you the usual
Dappled light drawing me on past the reading man,
As deeper and quieter we went, and all, all,
You, I, the reading man, the book, the day,
Were in the book; but not the birches.

To a Very Competent Young Lady

'. . . and she tried to curtsey as she spoke—fancy curtseying
as you're falling through the air! Do you think you could
manage it?'

ALICE'S ADVENTURES IN WONDERLAND

The years must have dropped away,
The paralysed body, the bottles, the trays,
The nurses, the staring out the window,
The me at your bedside.
The next day and the next day and the next.
Which had been your happiest?
I think an evening at the Met,
Rosenkavalier, the vast stage lit up
Yellow and grey and silver,
A silver rose expected, wonder in the air.
The next day and the next day and the next.
One morning at five o'clock at Pitié-Salpêtrière
Your silver clock stopped.
Tock.
Silencium.
Down, down, down.

You always did immediately
What circumstances called for.
Yes, I think
you managed it.

Snow Falling, Lady Murasaki Watching

At the window
of her simple home

she watches snow slowly falling
forming little hills in the garden.

Her husband whom she loved
dead a long while and still missed,

the Emperor's court its hypocrites and good souls
very far away.

A brown bird alights
shockingly alive in the snow.

Why am I still here? she thinks,
How will it all end?

Arthur Waley the translator stands
just outside of view

captures it
captures it.

*

I look up from my café table
at posters on which models

smiling insincerely endorse things
of which no one has the least need.

In the sky above a silver airplane
is on its way

where?

There are no reliable dates

to show when life began in this location.

There are no reliable dates
to show when the treaty—undated—was drawn up,
or was put into effect, or was subsequently
declared null and void, if declared null and void,
or, if still valid, stopped being honoured by both parties,
if stopped being honoured by both parties.

There are no reliable dates
to show when the ruins over there to the right
were first discovered embedded in Stratum 8A,
nor to show if Stratum 8A pre-dates the ruins
or if the ruins pre-date Stratum 8A.

There are no reliable dates
to show when you and I—if you and I, not you or I—
might have died, if indeed the and ever died,
if indeed and ever dies,
there are no reliable dates.

Tuba Mirum

I remember the day the girl
let go the day in Central Park.

Winter day, the park all white,
branches flashing, the sun a coin,
girl bundled up, walking,
running: no more unhappy mother,
no uncle daddy, no courts,
custody, clinics, cousins,
no more Alice, Holmes, Irene
Adler or other friends,
no more noise of buses through
distant dirty snow.

Only one thing to do, so she does it:
lets it go, lets it lift off—the day—
to where light lives, to where sound cracks
like the fragile crystal Mozart hears.

There she is: arms raised,
a plaid bundle on top of a mound.
The freedom of it!

Later, life mashed her.

I let go this poem, to follow her.

How Things Are

I opened my mouth to speak and all that
would come out were bits of coloured paper in

the wind I'd wanted to say 'I love you'
I'd wanted to say 'good-bye' I'd wanted to

say 'I'm sorry' I waved my arms wildly my

feet were immobile 'Hel' I started to
say but no use finishing it it came

out bits of coloured paper in the wind
and you everywhere and nowhere and it

was too little too late my tongue vibrated
wildly like a clapper and 'love' and 'good-bye'

and 'sorry' blew off it everywhere into
the wind and you in the stars now and there

never were nor ever are for any man
woman child or any book or brochure

any other words but these.

Patchwork Fields

Snow coming down, clouds of things.
Everything, everyone a cloud of things.
Meaning, a cloud of things.
Dreams, sly things.

Don't bruise her foot against a stone.
Angels, hold her up!

Couldn't lift a pin now, if it were given her.
Very heavy, pins.

Let the reins drop.
The horse knows the way home.

Dear Leo

Dear Leo, you haven't written in a while,
but honestly, I wasn't expecting you to.
I hope you are well. Sometimes I hope you don't
remember me, because there was pain attached to that.
I think pain may well outlive love, so best to forget
the whole package. What do I hope for you, Leo?
I hope you are the same kind of happy you were
when you were playing cribbage, when you were playing
golf, when you were listening to Brahms. I hope you don't
have to get up in the morning to go to someplace
you don't want to go to. I hope you don't feel like
my father any more, Leo, or anyone's.
The wise leave no writing behind, and then it is
up to us to read what they have not written.

My Mother's Birthday

May 4th. Each year she looks forward to it,
each year she's wary of it.
The garden snake at a birthday party, birthdays.
Never know which way they'll go.

Not your sweet old mum. Dress designer.
High living. Martinis and boyfriends all the way,
rumbas, flaming desserts. Poured into cabs at 4:00 a.m.,
home having captured—neat—the driver's life story.

Anyway, happy birthday! Cake, candles, pressies,
a few drinks, a few laughs, a prayer for cheer.
Happy birthday, Jeanie. 108 today.
'Thank you very much, I'd rather not.' So,

she didn't. Dead as a doornail at 84.
I'm going out to celebrate—Fellini's *Roma* and a long walk home.

RICHARD W. HALPERIN's work has been widely published since 2005, especially in *THE SHOp*, *Cyphers*, *Revival Literary Journal*, *The Stinging Fly* (featured poet, summer 2009), *Ambit*, *Carillon*, *The Delinquent*, *Obsessed with Pipework*. His debut collection is *Anniversary* (Salmon, 2010). A Japanese version appeared in 2012 (Sakiko Tagaki, translator; Kundai Bungei-sha Press, Tokyo, 2012). Several poems have been honoured in competitions in Ireland, the U.K. and Italy, including two 2012 first-prize poems in the present book. Mr. Halperin gave his first reading at Glenstal Abbey and has since read throughout Ireland, including at the Guinness Book of Records marathon, Irish Writers' Centre, Dublin. Prior to retirement as Chief of Section, UNESCO, he edited *Reading and Writing Poetry* (Paris, 2005), available *gratis* via the internet. He is currently working on a third collection *Quiet in a Quiet House*.